# THE MONEY-MINDED YOU

*A guide to earn, save, budget, and spend wisely*

## PATIENCE JOHN

Copyright © 2024 by Patience John

**All rights reserved**

No part of this publication may be reproduced, distributed, or transmitted in any form or by any means, including photocopying, recording, or other electronic or mechanical methods, without the prior written permission of the publisher, except in the case of brief quotations embodied in critical reviews and certain other non-commercial uses permitted by copyright law.

This is not the work of fiction but names, characters, places, and incidents either are the product of the author's imagination or are used fictitiously. Any resemblance to actual persons, living or dead, events, or locales is entirely coincidental

# The Money-Minded You

**3 | THE MONEY-MINDED YOU**

# TABLE OF CONTENT

INTRODUCTION ........................................................ 6
   Why This Book? ................................................ 6
   What You'll Gain .............................................. 6
   How This Book Works ........................................... 7
   Who This Book Is For .......................................... 8
CHAPTER 1 ............................................................. 9
   Shaping a Money-Minded Mentality .............................. 9
      Rethinking Money and Value ................................ 9
      Common Financial Pitfalls ................................. 9
      Cultivating a Growth-Oriented Financial Mindset .......... 10
      Goal Setting for Financial Success ....................... 10
CHAPTER 2 ............................................................ 12
   Boosting Your Income Potential ............................... 12
      Finding New Income Streams ............................... 12
      Turning Skills into Profits .............................. 12
      Exploring Gigs and Freelancing Options ................... 13
      Maximizing Your Time for Better Income ................... 13
CHAPTER 3 ............................................................ 14
   Budgeting Like a Pro ......................................... 14

Designing a Realistic Budget ............................ 14

Beyond Basics—Advanced Budgeting Tips . 14

Tracking Spending Effectively ..................... 15

Handling Budget Challenges ........................ 15

CHAPTER 4 ................................................................ 16

Mastering Saving Habits ............................... 16

Building an Emergency Fund ....................... 16

The Psychology Behind Saving .................... 17

Long-Term Financial Planning .................... 17

Introduction to Investments ......................... 18

CHAPTER 5 ................................................................ 19

Spending Wisely for a Wealthier Life ............... 19

Cutting Costs Without Sacrifice ................... 20

Negotiating for Better Deals ......................... 20

Aligning Expenses with Financial Goals ...... 21

CONCLUSION ......................................................... 22

# INTRODUCTION

## Why This Book?

In a world where money affects nearly every aspect of our lives, having a good handle on your finances isn't just important - it's empowering. You don't have to be wealthy or have a finance degree to start making wise money choices. Whether you're just starting out, managing family expenses, or looking to grow your savings, learning to earn, budget, save, and spend with intention can help you live with less stress and more confidence. This book is designed to make that journey clear, practical, and even enjoyable.

## What You'll Gain

By following the steps in each chapter, you'll gain skills that aren't just about money but also about creating a life that aligns with your values and goals. You'll learn how to: Build a mindset that helps you stay on top of your finances and make smart decisions.

Discover income opportunities that suit your lifestyle and skill set.

Set up a budget that works with your needs, not against them.

Save consistently, no matter your income level, so you're ready for anything.

Spend in ways that support your goals instead of setting you back.

## How This Book Works

Each chapter focuses on a major part of financial health: earning, budgeting, saving, and spending. I'll break down each topic into steps, share practical examples, and give you tools to try out. Don't worry about having a background in finance—each idea is explained in plain language, with simple steps you can take right away.

As you move through this book, keep in mind that even small changes in how you handle your money can lead to big improvements over time. You don't need to be perfect, and you don't have to follow every piece of advice exactly. This book is here to help you build a money-minded approach that works best for you.

## Who This Book Is For

**The Money Minded You** is for anyone who wants to live with financial stability and confidence, no matter where they're starting from. Maybe you're just starting to earn and feel a bit lost. Maybe you've been managing your own finances for years but feel like you could do better. This book will meet you where you are and give you the tools to reach the financial life you want.

# CHAPTER 1

## Shaping a Money-Minded Mentality

### Rethinking Money and Value

Money is a tool, but many of us get caught up in seeing it as something more complicated or elusive. To build a money-minded mentality, start by thinking about what money actually does for you, it allows you to meet your needs, enjoy life, and build security. By viewing money as a tool, you can focus on using it purposefully, not emotionally. This shift in mindset is key to making confident financial choices.

### Common Financial Pitfalls

We all have habits that, without realizing it, chip away at our financial health. Maybe it's spending on small things every day or avoiding a budget because it seems restrictive. These habits are easy to fall into but can keep you stuck. This section will help you identify where your money leaks might be and how small changes can make a big difference. For example, setting aside a set amount for "fun" spending can help you stay within limits while still enjoying life.

## Cultivating a Growth-Oriented Financial Mindset

Developing a financial growth mindset means thinking about how you can make your money work for you. This isn't just about earning more- it's about using what you have wisely and believing that your financial situation can improve. Start by setting one small financial goal, like saving $100 by the end of the month. Small wins build confidence and show that progress is possible.

## Goal Setting for Financial Success

Setting goals gives your money a purpose and makes it easier to stick to financial plans. When setting goals, be specific, don't just say, "I want to save more." Instead, try "I want to save $500 in three months for an emergency fund." Break it down even further to set aside $40 a week. Practical, small goals like these make the bigger ones feel achievable. And with each goal you meet, you'll strengthen your "money-minded" approach.

This chapter will help readers reshape their relationship with money, focusing on clear, achievable steps that build a stronger, more confident financial mindset.

# CHAPTER 2

## Boosting Your Income Potential

### Finding New Income Streams

When it comes to earning more, think beyond your regular paycheck. Today, there are plenty of ways to bring in extra money, whether you have a lot of free time or just a little. You could consider freelance work, selling handmade items, or starting a small online store. These extra income streams don't have to take up all your time - they're about creating multiple ways to make money, even in small amounts, to support your main income.

### Turning Skills into Profits

You might already have skills that others are willing to pay for. Maybe you're good at writing, designing, organizing, or cooking - almost any skill can be turned into a service or product. Think about what you enjoy doing or something you're good at. Then, look for opportunities where these skills could help others. For example, if you're great with organization, you could help people set up efficient home offices or organize their schedules. The key is to recognize your unique abilities and think creatively about ways to use them to make money.

## Exploring Gigs and Freelancing Options

Freelance platforms and gig economy jobs are flexible, making it easier to earn without a long-term commitment. You can choose projects that fit your schedule and skill level. From online tutoring to delivery gigs, there's something for nearly everyone. Set a specific time each week to work on these gigs, so it doesn't interfere with your primary job or personal life. Freelancing and gig work can be a great way to add extra income without too much risk.

## Maximizing Your Time for Better Income

It's easy to feel like you're too busy to take on extra work, but small time adjustments can make a big difference. Track how you currently spend your time, then look for "gaps" where you can add focused work sessions. This could mean using an hour in the evening or part of your weekend to work on a side project or gig. The goal is to make use of pockets of free time without burning out. Working smarter, not longer, helps you balance extra income with your well-being.

# CHAPTER 3

## Budgeting Like a Pro

### Designing a Realistic Budget

Creating a budget isn't just about limiting what you spend; it's about building a clear, realistic plan for your money that lets you cover your needs, save for the future, and enjoy the present. Start by listing your income sources and then map out your regular expenses - rent, groceries, utilities, transportation, and any debts. Once you know where your money goes each month, you can adjust spending in areas where you might be overspending and find a balance that aligns with your goals.

### Beyond Basics—Advanced Budgeting Tips

Once you've got the basics down, there are simple ways to make budgeting even more effective. The 50/30/20 rule, for example, is a popular approach that breaks down your income: 50% for needs, 30% for wants, and 20% for savings or paying down debt. Adjusting these percentages can make the plan more flexible for your needs. Another option is the cash envelope system - setting aside specific cash amounts for categories like groceries or entertainment, so you don't accidentally overspend. Try these methods and see which fits your style best.

## Tracking Spending Effectively

Keeping an eye on your spending is key to sticking with your budget. Simple apps like Mint, YNAB, or even a basic spreadsheet can help you track where your money is going. By logging your expenses daily or weekly, you'll avoid the shock of realizing you've gone over budget at the end of the month. Tracking can also help you spot patterns - like buying too many takeout meals or impulsive online purchases - that you might want to cut back on.

## Handling Budget Challenges

Even with the best intentions, life sometimes throws curveballs. Maybe your car breaks down, or you face unexpected medical bills. When things get tough, don't be hard on yourself. Focus on adapting your budget: pause any non-essential spending, look for areas to trim, and try to avoid dipping into savings if possible. Remember, a budget isn't set in stone; it's a tool to help you, not restrict you. Be flexible, and make changes as needed to stay on track.

# CHAPTER 4

## Mastering Saving Habits

Saving money may sound simple, but it's a skill that requires focus, consistency, and a little creativity. In this chapter, we'll go over practical, manageable ways to make saving a natural part of your life. From preparing for emergencies to planning for future goals, these habits will help you build a strong financial foundation.

### Building an Emergency Fund

Think of an emergency fund as a financial safety net. Life can be unpredictable - a medical bill, car repair, or sudden job change could throw your budget off course. Aim to save at least three to six months' worth of basic expenses. Start small; even setting aside $10 or $20 a week can build up over time. Automate this process by setting up a recurring transfer from your checking to your savings account so you're building that fund effortlessly.

## The Psychology Behind Saving

Saving doesn't have to feel like a punishment. One way to make it enjoyable is to focus on what you're gaining rather than what you're giving up. Picture yourself debt-free, or imagine the peace of mind of having enough for emergencies. Set mini-rewards for reaching savings milestones - like treating yourself to a small gift after hitting your first $500. This way, you're reinforcing positive behavior and making saving a rewarding experience.

## Long-Term Financial Planning

Savings aren't just for short-term needs; they're also crucial for larger life goals. Whether it's buying a home, funding education, or taking a dream vacation, having a savings plan in place keeps you on track. Break down big goals into smaller, achievable steps. For example, if you want to save $5,000 for a future goal, divide that by the months you have to save, and commit to setting aside that amount each month. Staying organized and focused helps make even the biggest goals feel doable.

### Introduction to Investments

Saving is a great start, but putting some of your money to work through investing can help it grow faster over time. If you're new to investing, start with something simple, like a high-yield savings account or a low-risk investment fund. Even a small amount - like $50 per month - can make a difference over the years. Before diving in, learn about your options and risks, and don't hesitate to seek advice from a financial professional if you feel unsure. Investing doesn't have to be complicated, but it can help you reach your financial goals faster.

# CHAPTER 5

## Spending Wisely for a Wealthier Life

In this chapter, we'll focus on practical ways to make the most of your money by spending wisely. Smart spending doesn't mean cutting out all the fun; it's about being intentional with where your money goes. Let's dive into strategies that can help you feel good about your purchases, reduce unnecessary expenses, and make sure each dollar supports your long-term financial goals.

### Developing Smart Spending Habits

Smart spending starts with a simple question: "Do I really need this, or do I just want it?" It's okay to spend on things you enjoy, but recognizing the difference between needs and wants is essential. When a purchase is more of a "want," consider waiting a day or two before buying it. This pause often helps us see what's truly worth our money - and what we can skip.

### Cutting Costs Without Sacrifice

Saving money doesn't mean giving up everything you love. Instead, look for ways to keep the things you enjoy but at a lower cost. For instance, if you love going out to eat, try setting a monthly dining budget or explore happy hours where you can enjoy a meal for less. Small changes like switching to a more affordable phone plan, cutting down subscriptions you don't use, or buying in bulk can add up to big savings over time without feeling like a sacrifice.

### Negotiating for Better Deals

Negotiation isn't just for car sales or job offers - it's something you can use in many areas of life. Call your service providers, like internet or insurance companies, and ask if there are better rates or promotions available. Often, companies are willing to work with you to keep you as a customer. The same goes for high-interest loans or credit cards; sometimes, simply asking for a lower rate can save you money. Be polite, but don't be afraid to ask.

## Aligning Expenses with Financial Goals

Every purchase you make should bring you closer to your financial goals. Before spending on something big, ask yourself how it aligns with what you want in the future. For example, if your goal is to save for a vacation, think twice about spending extra on takeout or new clothes that month. It's all about trade-offs - small adjustments today make your bigger goals more achievable tomorrow. Keeping your goals in mind will make it easier to stay on track without feeling restricted.

## CONCLUSION

Congratulations on taking this journey to become **The Money Minded You**. By now, you've explored how to make smarter financial decisions, from earning more and budgeting better to saving consistently and spending wisely. Each chapter has given you the tools you need to build a stable financial future, but remember, the key to financial success lies in consistency and making informed choices every day.

Start by setting clear goals. Financial growth is most achievable when you know exactly what you're aiming for. Maybe it's creating an emergency fund, paying off debt, or growing your income through side gigs. Pick one goal at a time, stay focused, and celebrate every small step forward.

Next, remember that budgeting is your biggest ally. It's not about restricting yourself but about giving each dollar a job. The goal is to spend on what you value and to cut out the rest. Adjust your budget as your needs change, and don't hesitate to refine your approach if something isn't working.

Saving, too, is a habit that builds with time. Start small, automate where you can, and add to your savings regularly. You'll be amazed at how small, consistent contributions grow over time. And as your savings grow, don't forget to consider safe ways to invest, even if it's in small amounts. Building wealth isn't about getting rich quickly; it's about making thoughtful decisions over the long term.

Finally, spend with intention. You don't have to cut out every joy in life, but aim to make purchases that add real value. Prioritize spending that aligns with your goals, and avoid debt for things that lose value quickly.

Becoming money-minded is a journey, not a destination. Along the way, there will be successes and challenges, but with the right mindset, you're well-prepared to navigate both. Embrace each step, and stay committed. Remember, every positive financial choice you make brings you closer to a more secure, balanced, and fulfilling life.

Here's to a financially empowered future!

# THE END

www.ingramcontent.com/pod-product-compliance
Lightning Source LLC
Chambersburg PA
CBHW030046230526
45472CB00005B/1705